Play Sport!

By Julie Haydon

T0342785

Contents

A World of Sport

Many people play sport.

Some sports you can do on your own.
Running is a sport you can do on your own.

Some sports are played in a team.
Hockey is a team sport.

Team members often wear uniforms.
The uniforms make it easy
to see who is on each team.

Some sports need special equipment.

Soccer is played with a soccer ball.
The players also wear special boots.

Some sports are played in special places.

Tennis is played on a tennis court.
There is a net in the middle of the court.

Some sports are water sports.

Swimming is a water sport.
These girls are having a swimming race
in a swimming pool.

These men are playing basketball.
Basketball is their job.
The men are trying to win the game.

Some people play sport as a job.
Some people play sport to keep fit.

But most people play sport
because it is fun.

Be Healthy, Play Sport!

By Dr Smith

I think children should play sport every day so that they stay healthy.

Sport helps children keep fit.
Children use their bodies when they play sport.
This helps them to be strong and healthy.

Sport is lots of fun for children.
Many sports are games.
Children enjoy playing games.
Games are a good way
for children to learn new skills, too.

Sport is a good way for children to make new friends.

Children meet lots of new people when they play sport.

They learn to play well with others, too.

Sport is a good way for children to learn about winning and losing. Children learn that it is fun to win, but it is all right to lose, too.

Sport is a good way for children to learn about rules.
Everyone has to learn how to follow rules.

Children should play sport every day.
It is fun, and it is good for them.